BUILDING
BIG
GREEN
ARCHITECTURE

by Joyce Markovics

CHERRY LAKE PRESS
cherrylakepublishing.com

CHERRY LAKE PRESS

Published in the United States of America by Cherry Lake Publishing Group
Ann Arbor, Michigan
www.cherrylakepublishing.com

Reading Adviser: Beth Walker Gambro, MS, Ed., Reading Consultant, Yorkville, IL
Content Adviser: Jeffrey Shumaker, AICP, Urban Designer, Planner, Architect, and Educator
Book Designer: Ed Morgan

Photo Credits: Photo Credits: unsplash.com/Ricardo Gomez Angel, cover; unsplash.com/Sido
Lee, title page; unsplash.com/Matteo Flamino, 5; Wikimedia Commons/Forgemind ArchMedia,
6; Wikimedia Commons/V.albani, 7; unsplash.com/Daniel Sessler, 8-9; freepik.com, 10; unsplash.
com/David Close, 11; unsplash.com/Patrick Hunt, 12-13; © Phillip Harrington/Alamy Stock Photo, 13
inset; © MARKA/Alamy Stock Photo, 14; © Inigo Bujedo Aguirre-VIEW/Alamy Stock Photo, 15; unsplash.
com/Lisa Yount, 16; Wikimedia Commons/Kshitij Charania, 17; Wikimedia Commons/Anselmrogers,
18; Wikimedia Commons/Elbowmacaroni, 19; freepik.com, 20-21; © Arcaid Images/Alamy Stock Photo,
22-23; © Agarianna76/Shutterstock, 24; freepik.com, 25; © atiger/Shutterstock, 26; © Norman
Allchin/Shutterstock, 27.

Cherry Lake Press is an imprint of Cherry Lake Publishing Group.

Library of Congress Cataloging-in-Publication Data

Names: Markovics, Joyce L., author.
Title: Green architecture / by Joyce Markovics.
Description: Ann Arbor, Michigan : Cherry Lake Publishing, [2023] | Series:
  Building big : amazing architecture | Includes bibliographical
  references and index. | Audience: Grades 4-6
Identifiers: LCCN 2022039594 (print) | LCCN 2022039595 (ebook) | ISBN
  9781668919835 (hardcover) | ISBN 9781668920855 (paperback) | ISBN
  9781668923511 (adobe pdf) | ISBN 9781668922187 (ebook) | ISBN
  9781668924846 (kindle edition) | ISBN 9781668926178 (epub)
Subjects: LCSH: Sustainable architecture—Juvenile literature.
Classification: LCC NA2542.36 .M26 2023 (print) | LCC NA2542.36 (ebook) |
  DDC 720/.47—dc23/eng/20220822
LC record available at https://lccn.loc.gov/2022039594
LC ebook record available at https://lccn.loc.gov/2022039595

Printed in the United States of America
Corporate Graphics

CONTENTS

Plant Power

In Milan, Italy, there are two apartment buildings wrapped in what looks like shaggy green blankets. The "blankets" are, in fact, thousands of trees, shrubs, and other plants! The 260- and 360-foot (79- and 110-meter) towers are called *Bosco Verticale* in Italian. This term means "**Vertical** Forest." Italian architect Stefano Boeri came up with the concept for the plant-covered buildings. At first, the idea seemed crazy to the developer of the towers. But he was also intrigued by Boeri's vision. "I had my **obsession** with trees since I was a kid," Boeri shared. He said he was inspired by a 1957 book called *The Baron in the Trees*. It's about a young man who climbs a tree and lives the rest of his life there. Boeri had an image of people in their homes "**observing** the world through the **filter** of leaves and branches," he said.

FACT BOX

An architect is a person who designs buildings. Architecture is the art of designing buildings. Architects use different elements to express their vision for a building. For example, they consider location, shape, size, materials, and other factors.

Bosco Verticale was completed in 2014 in Milan, Italy.

In full support of Boeri's design, the developer began constructing the towers. The architect not only set out to provide comfortable homes for people in the crowded city. Boeri also wanted to help clean Milan's air. He knew that trees and other plants are one of the best ways to absorb carbon dioxide, a **greenhouse gas**. Greenhouse gases contribute to **climate change** and the warming of the planet plus more extreme weather. Trees fight climate change and in the process produce oxygen for people to breathe.

Here a large tree is being lifted by a crane to be placed on one of the buildings.

In addition, Boeri designed the towers knowing the trees and plants would block the Sun's light. This would help keep the apartments cool on hot days. The plants would also provide a barrier to the wind. Plus, they would **muffle** the sounds of the noisy city. Boeri's concept included more than 90 kinds of plants, which he called "a family." He knew such a big variety of plants would attract many birds and insects to the buildings and city.

Architect Stefano Boeri

The two buildings include about 800 trees, 5,000 shrubs, and 11,000 smaller plants. They were lifted into place using cranes and other machines.

Boeri also placed solar panels on the two towers. Solar power is the energy given off by the Sun. The solar panels use this energy to make electricity to power the building. That's not all. Boeri created a way to collect the wastewater, filter it, and use it to water the many thousands of plants. When the buildings were finished, people were in awe. The vertical forest idea was a hit, inspiring similar projects around the world.

One of Boeri's newest and biggest projects is a vertical green city in Mexico. It will cover 362 acres (146 hectares) and include 120,000 plants! "It's very important to completely change how these new cities are developing. . . . That means parks, it means gardens, but it also means having buildings with trees," said Boeri. "I want to bring more trees to the city and more humans to the forest. Forests need our help to take better care of them and we need trees to take better care of us," he said.

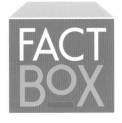

The *Bosco Verticale* plants are watered using an **irrigation** system that runs throughout the two towers. Workers called "flying gardeners" use special **harnesses** to climb the buildings to care for the plants.

What Is Green Architecture?

All buildings are created using architecture, a combination of science and art. But not all buildings use green, or **sustainable**, architecture. This type of architecture focuses on not wasting energy and other resources. People have **depleted** Earth's resources over time. Some of these resources, such as **fossil fuels**, cannot be replaced. Fossil fuels also pollute the environment and worsen climate change. But there are renewable energy sources that don't harm the planet and cannot be used up. These include solar and wind power.

Green architects want to help the environment and improve the quality of life for the people who use the buildings they design.

Architects who design green buildings also carefully consider the materials they use. Traditional building materials include stone, wood, steel, concrete, and **synthetics**. They often create a lot of waste. Some green designs use **recycled** or environmentally friendly materials like bamboo or mushrooms. These make far less waste. Finally, green architects think about the location of a building and how it affects the environment. They come up with ways to make the best use out of the Sun or shade to heat or cool the building, for example.

A bamboo forest

Bamboo grows quickly, is very strong, and makes a highly sustainable building material. It can be used to build homes, bridges, and even furniture.

During the 1960s, architects first began seriously thinking about sustainable architecture. Before that time, there was little concern about pollution or using up Earth's resources. Things changed when scientists realized humans were causing lasting damage to the environment. That's when architects started designing buildings that would have less of an impact on the environment. These architects included an American named Buckminster Fuller. He introduced a lightweight, strong, and energy-efficient structure called a geodesic (jee-uh-DES-ik) dome. The dome could be easily assembled and made in big and small sizes. Fuller believed in "doing more with less" to help the environment. However, Fuller's and other architects' green designs never became widely popular. At the same time as they were working, the demand for houses and other buildings grew. Many of these structures were built using materials that harmed the environment. They also used up lots of nonrenewable resources and created waste.

A geodesic dome

Any building can be a green building. For example, a home, office, school, or hospital can be a green building as long as it meets certain "green" standards.

Buckminster Fuller holds a model of a sphere he invented.

Despite the efforts of early supporters, green architecture was slow to catch on. By the 21st century, the construction **industry** was using up a huge amount of the planet's resources. On top of that, it was creating up to 50 percent of the garbage in landfills. And it was also responsible for nearly 30 percent of all greenhouse gas **emissions**.

This building in Italy was designed by William McDonough.

FACT BOX

Any building can be green or LEED-certified. For example, a home, office, school, or even a hospital can be a green building as long as it meets certain standards.

As a reaction to this, the green movement grew stronger. Architects called for more sustainable designs. And some businesses did too. Architect William McDonough was one of the early leaders of the movement. He believes in buildings that do no harm—and that can actually benefit the environment over time. From small businesses to factories, McDonough has designed dozens of buildings. Many of them are LEED **certified**. LEED is a system for rating buildings based on how sustainable they are.

McDonough is known for creating green roofs made from living plants. This building in Barcelona, Spain, has solar panels on its roof and captures rainwater to reuse.

The First Green Structures

Many green architects were influenced by ancient and **Indigenous** architecture. Long ago, Indigenous people designed buildings and other structures that worked in **harmony** with nature. They saw themselves as part of their environment, not separate from it. For example, the Anasazi people in the southwestern United States built their villages on cliffs out of clay bricks. In turn, the clay absorbed the Sun's heat to warm their homes. In colder northern areas, the Inuit people carved dome-shaped dwellings out of snow and ice. The snow acted as an **insulator** and kept the people inside comfortable.

This Anasazi cliff dwelling in Colorado was built around the year 1190.

A highly decorated stepwell in Patan in the state of Gujarat, India

In ancient India, people built stone stepwells. The wells had four walls with stairs that led deep into the earth. The structures held groundwater that people could only access by climbing the stairs. The stepwells provided water during droughts and places for people to cool off on hot days.

This is an example of a Khasi living tree root bridge. The area of India where the Khasi people live receives between 32 and 45 feet (10 and 14 m) of rainfall a year!

In another part of India, the Khasi people have been turning living trees into bridges and ladders for hundreds of years. The place where they live is one of the wettest on Earth. Floods are common. So the Khasi use nature to help them! They do this by training fig tree roots to grow across rivers and streams. The roots eventually **intertwine** to make a bridge that people can walk on. It can take decades for the bridges to fully come together. However, when they do, they're the perfect architectural solution to crossing a flooded waterway.

In addition to living bridges, the Khasi place their homes on hilltops where it's drier. They often use bamboo as a building material. The Khasi design their bamboo homes off the ground so rainwater can flow under them. Architect and professor Julia Watson has studied the Khasi and other Indigenous people around the world. She urges architects to **embrace** the wisdom of these Indigenous designs. She sees this as an important step in improving humans' relationship with nature, especially as climate change makes Earth less **hospitable**.

The Khasi people have adapted to the environment without harming it.

Human activity, including the burning of fossil fuels, has caused temperatures around the world to rise higher and faster than ever before. This has led to more floods, fires, and droughts.

Green Buildings Around the World

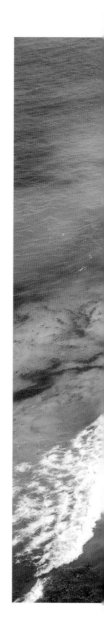

Today, there are many architects around the world who are designing with nature and sustainability in mind. Eduardo "Roth" Neira is a Mexico-based architect. He uses natural materials and **techniques** to build bold, curving structures. Many look like they're straight out of a fairytale. "Nature is my school," he said. "You see in nature there are not square angles. . . . But in life, we live in square places."

Roth works with Indigenous Mayan people in Mexico to build his creations. One such place is an artist's community, gallery, and home in the jungle. "We couldn't bring heavy machines," said Roth. So everything is made by hand. And trees are a key part of the design. "There are 200 trees living in this house," Roth said. He also uses sustainable vines to form tunnels and walkways. "We work with **organic** materials that avoid environmental impact," said Roth. In his work, he seeks to "honor the forms of the soil, to coexist with the trees" as well as respect the people who came before us.

This is an aerial view of Roth's luxury hotel, Azulik, in Tulum, Mexico. Trees and vines grow in and around the buildings.

FACT BOX

Roth has designed everything from bridges and walkways to houses and hotels.

Other green architects incorporate cutting-edge **technology** into their designs. Several architects worked together to design a building for the National University of Singapore. The six-story building is a net-zero-energy structure. That means it makes all of its own energy. Sometimes, it makes extra energy—up to 30 percent **surplus**. This is called being energy positive. The building achieves this with more than 1,200 solar panels on its large roof. The building also has a special cooling system with fans that **circulate** the cool air. This system is 20 percent more efficient than standard air conditioning. The building is also beautiful. It has an open design that allows students to easily move through it. There are green spaces where students can study and hang out too.

FACT BOX

Net-zero architecture has the least impact on the environment. These buildings make all of the power they need.

This is the National University of Singapore's zero-energy building. Singapore is a country in Southeast Asia.

Green architecture can also transform waste into something useful. In Côte d'Ivoire (koht dee-VWAR), a country in West Africa, hundreds of tons of plastic trash are created each day. Only a tiny percentage of that trash is recycled. UNICEF, the United Nations Children's Fund, created a competition to solve the plastic waste problem—and help kids in the process. They connected with Conceptos Plásticos, a company in Colombia, South America. The company recycles plastic into large bricks that look like Legos! The bricks can then be used to build schools, homes, and other structures.

In the West African country of Gambia, people use recycled plastic bottles filled with sand to construct the walls of a building.

Green architecture is giving children in Africa more access to education.

According to UNICEF, more than 1 million children in Côte d'Ivoire don't go to school. One reason is a lack of space. There simply aren't enough classrooms. In 2018, UNICEF built classrooms using the recycled bricks. The children now had more space to move around and learn. "People couldn't believe the classrooms were made of plastic," said a teacher. UNICEF has plans to build hundreds more of these green classrooms.

A Greener Future

Buildings of all sizes can be sustainable. One of the world's tallest buildings is also one of the greenest! China's Shanghai Tower rises a whopping 2,073 feet (632 m). It's covered by two exterior layers that allow for better **ventilation**. The skyscraper has 270 **turbines** that use the wind's energy to power the lights. In all, it uses 80 percent less energy than similar towers.

The Shanghai Tower in China

In contrast, the Pixel Building is a small office building in Australia. On its roof it has wind turbines, live plants, and a system to capture rainwater. The building's most striking feature is colorful exterior panels that keep the interior cool. Green architecture can take this and many other forms. To effect real change, people need to embrace all of the forms today and in the future. "Architecture has a critical responsibility in the future of human beings," said Roth.

The Pixel Building was built using recycled and sustainable materials.

Design a
Green Building

Think about what you just learned about green architecture in this book. Now use that information to design your own green building!

DESIGN CONCEPT: What is your idea for your building? Where will it be located? What will it be used for? What green materials will you use to build it? Think about all the ways you can make your building sustainable.

PLAN: Think about what the exterior and interior of your building will look like. Will it have solar panels or other green features? How will it fit into the landscape? How big or small will it be?

DRAW: Grab some paper and a pencil. Sketch the floor plan of your building to show the arrangement of rooms. Label each room. Next, draw the exterior, noting what materials will be used.

BUILD A MODEL: Use materials around your home, such as paper, cardboard, scissors, straws, popsicle sticks, and glue, to build a small model of your building.

REFINE YOUR PLAN: What works about your design? What doesn't work? Make any needed changes to improve your building.

GLOSSARY

certified (SUR-tuh-fyed) having met the official requirements to do a specific job

circulate (SUR-kyuh-leyt) to move freely in a closed system

climate change (KLYE-mit CHAYNJ) the warming of Earth's air and oceans due to environmental changes, such as a buildup of greenhouse gases that trap the Sun's heat in Earth's atmosphere

depleted (dih-PLEET-uhd) used up

embrace (em-BREYS) to accept willingly

emissions (ih-MISH-uhnz) substances such as gases and soot released into the air by fuelburning engines

filter (FIL-tur) to pass through something

fossil fuels (FOSS-uhl FYOO-uhlz) fuels such as coal, oil, and natural gas made from the remains of plants and animals that died millions of years ago

greenhouse gas (GREEN-houss GAS) a gas such as carbon dioxide or methane that traps warm air in the atmosphere; responsible for global warming

harmony (HAHR-muh-nee) in agreement with to form a consistent whole

harnesses (HAR-niss-iz) captures

hospitable (HOS-pi-tuh-buhl) pleasant for living in

indigenous (in-DIJ-uh-nuhss) relating to people originating from a particular place

industry (IN-duh-stree) an area of business

insulator (IN-suh-layt-ur) materials that

intertwine (in-ter-TWAHYN) to twist together

irrigation (ir-ih-GEY-shun) using water to grow things

muffle (MUHF-uhl) to deaden the sound of something

observing (uhb-ZURV-ing) watching and noticing something

obsession (uhb-SESH-uhn) the state of being fixed on something

organic (or-GAN-ik) a material that was once living, such as wood

recycled (ree-SYE-kuhld) when unwanted materials are turned into something useful

surplus (SUR-pluhs) something that remains above what is used or needed

sustainable (suh-STAYN-uh-buhl) a way of living that does not use up nonrenewable resources; living in a way that can be continued forever

synthetics (sin-THET-iks) things made by humans using chemicals that may be harmful

techniques (tek-NEEKS) the ways of carrying out particular tasks

technology (tek-NOL-uh-jee) useful things created by science

turbines (TUR-byenz) machines that are powered by wind

ventilation (ven-tuh-LAY-shun) something providing fresh air to an indoor space

vertical (VUR-tuh-kuhl) in an up-and-down

READ MORE

Allen, Peter. *Atlas of Amazing Architecture*. London: Cicada Books, 2021.

Armstrong, Simon. *Cool Architecture*. London: Pavilion, 2015.

Dillon, Patrick. *The Story of Buildings*. Somerville, MA: Candlewick Press, 2014.

Glancey, Jonathan. *Architecture: A Visual History*. London: DK, 2021.

Moreno, Mark. *Architecture for Kids*. Emeryville, VA: Rockridge Press, 2021.

LEARN MORE ONLINE

Architecture for Children
https://archforkids.com

Britannica Kids: Architecture
https://kids.britannica.com/students/article/architecture/272939

Center for Architecture: Architecture at Home Resources
https://www.centerforarchitecture.org/k-12/resources/

Lego Design Challenge
https://www.architects.org/uploads/BSA_LWW_LEGO_Challenge.pdf

STEAM Exercises: Kid Architecture
http://www.vancebm.com/kidArchitect/pages/steamExercises.html

INDEX

ABOUT THE AUTHOR

Joyce Markovics has written hundreds of books for young readers. She lives in a nearly 200-year-old carpenter Gothic style house along the Hudson River. Joyce would like to thank architect, designer, and city planner Jeff Shumaker for his insight and help creating this series.